LOOK INSIDE
CROSS-SECTIONS
PLANES

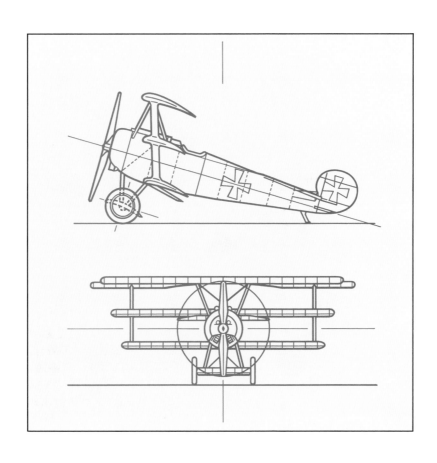

LOOK INSIDE
CROSS-SECTIONS
PLANES

ILLUSTRATED BY
HANS JENSSEN

WRITTEN BY
MICHAEL JOHNSTONE

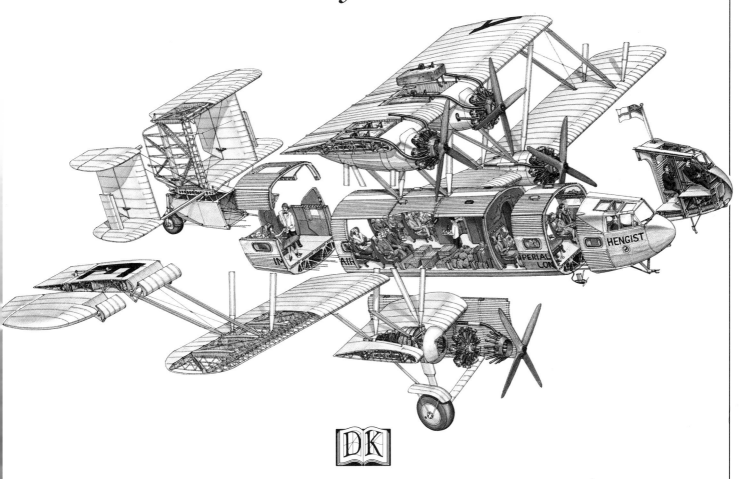

DK

DORLING KINDERSLEY
LONDON • NEW YORK • STUTTGART

A DORLING KINDERSLEY BOOK

Art Editor Dorian Spencer Davies
Designer Sharon Grant
Senior Art Editor C. David Gillingwater
Senior Editor John C. Miles
U.S. Assistant Editor Camela Decaire
Production Ruth Cobb
Consultant Andrew Nahum
The Science Museum, London

First American edition, 1994
2 4 6 8 10 9 7 5 3
Published in the United States
by Dorling Kindersley Publishing, Inc.,
95 Madison Avenue, New York, New York 10016

Library of Congress Cataloging - in - Publication Data
Johnstone, Michael.
Planes / written by Michael Johnstone;
illustrated by Hans Jenssen. – 1st American ed.
p. cm. – (Look inside cross-sections)
Includes index.
ISBN 1-56458-520-4
1. Airplanes – Design and construction – Juvenile literature.
[1. Airplanes – Design and construction.]
I. Jenssen. Hans, 1963-, ill.
II. Title. III. Series.
TL547. J575 1994
629. 133'34 – dc20   93 – 46373
                                              CIP
                                              AC

Reproduced by Dot Gradations. Essex
Printed and bound by Proost, Belgium

CONTENTS

TRIPLANE

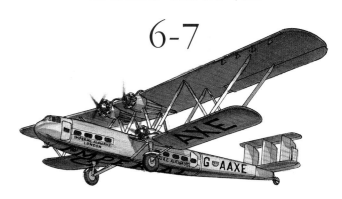

HANDLEY PAGE

BOEING 314

SPITFIRE

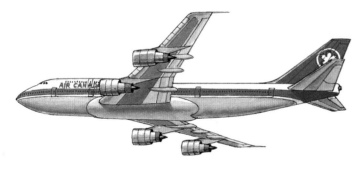

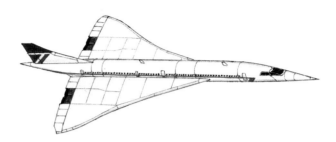
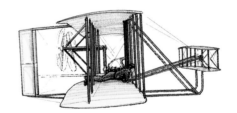

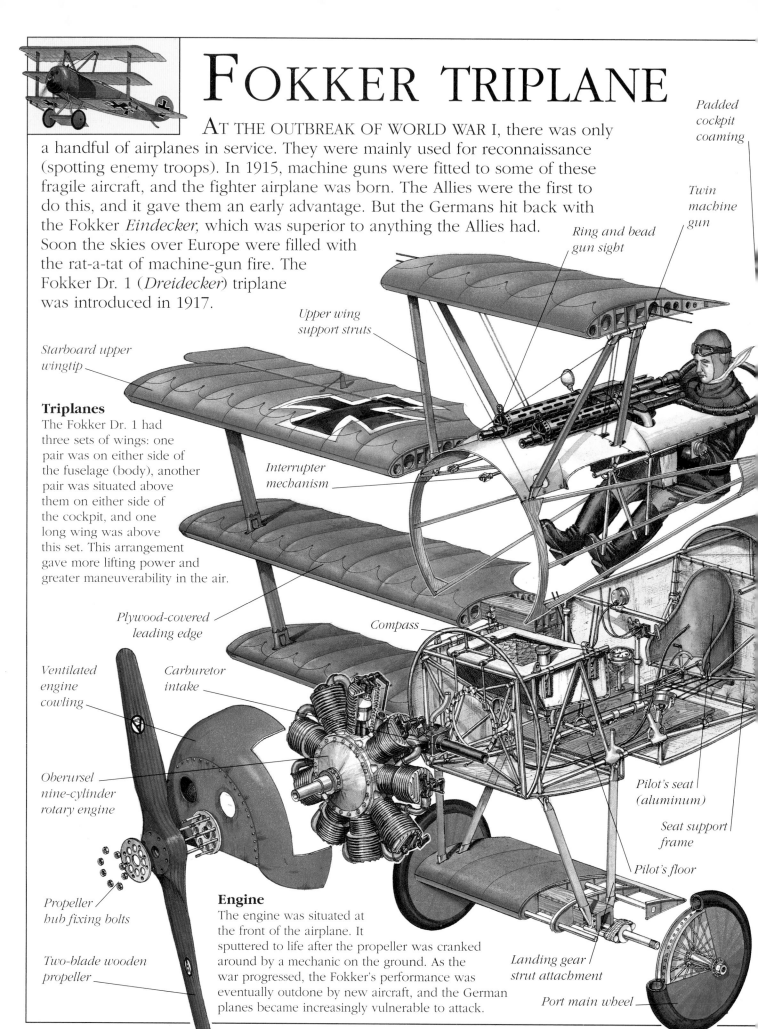

FOKKER TRIPLANE

AT THE OUTBREAK OF WORLD WAR I, there was only a handful of airplanes in service. They were mainly used for reconnaissance (spotting enemy troops). In 1915, machine guns were fitted to some of these fragile aircraft, and the fighter airplane was born. The Allies were the first to do this, and it gave them an early advantage. But the Germans hit back with the Fokker *Eindecker,* which was superior to anything the Allies had. Soon the skies over Europe were filled with the rat-a-tat of machine-gun fire. The Fokker Dr. 1 (*Dreidecker*) triplane was introduced in 1917.

Padded cockpit coaming

Twin machine gun

Ring and bead gun sight

Upper wing support struts

Starboard upper wingtip

Triplanes
The Fokker Dr. 1 had three sets of wings: one pair was on either side of the fuselage (body), another pair was situated above them on either side of the cockpit, and one long wing was above this set. This arrangement gave more lifting power and greater maneuverability in the air.

Interrupter mechanism

Plywood-covered leading edge

Compass

Ventilated engine cowling

Carburetor intake

Oberursel nine-cylinder rotary engine

Pilot's seat (aluminum)

Seat support frame

Pilot's floor

Propeller hub fixing bolts

Two-blade wooden propeller

Engine
The engine was situated at the front of the airplane. It sputtered to life after the propeller was cranked around by a mechanic on the ground. As the war progressed, the Fokker's performance was eventually outdone by new aircraft, and the German planes became increasingly vulnerable to attack.

Landing gear strut attachment

Port main wheel

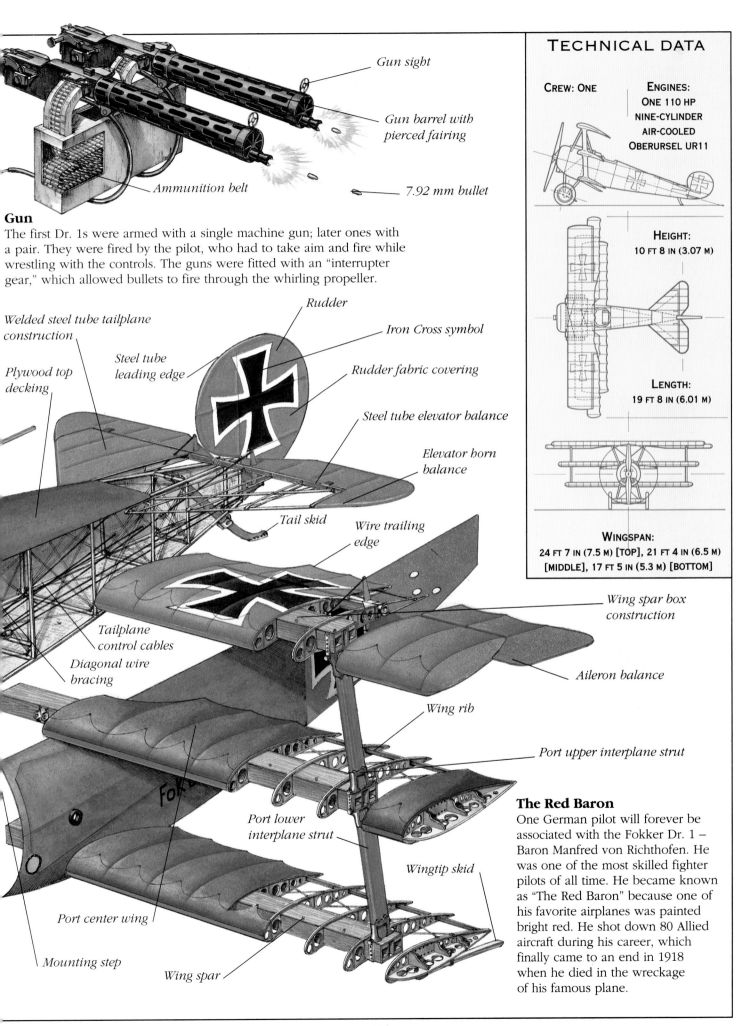

Gun sight

Gun barrel with pierced fairing

Ammunition belt

7.92 mm bullet

Gun

The first Dr. 1s were armed with a single machine gun; later ones with a pair. They were fired by the pilot, who had to take aim and fire while wrestling with the controls. The guns were fitted with an "interrupter gear," which allowed bullets to fire through the whirling propeller.

Welded steel tube tailplane construction

Plywood top decking

Steel tube leading edge

Rudder

Iron Cross symbol

Rudder fabric covering

Steel tube elevator balance

Elevator horn balance

Tail skid

Wire trailing edge

Tailplane control cables

Diagonal wire bracing

Wing spar box construction

Aileron balance

Wing rib

Port upper interplane strut

Port lower interplane strut

Wingtip skid

Port center wing

Mounting step

Wing spar

TECHNICAL DATA

CREW: ONE

ENGINES:
ONE 110 HP
NINE-CYLINDER
AIR-COOLED
OBERURSEL UR11

HEIGHT:
10 FT 8 IN (3.07 M)

LENGTH:
19 FT 8 IN (6.01 M)

WINGSPAN:
24 FT 7 IN (7.5 M) [TOP], 21 FT 4 IN (6.5 M)
[MIDDLE], 17 FT 5 IN (5.3 M) [BOTTOM]

The Red Baron

One German pilot will forever be associated with the Fokker Dr. 1 – Baron Manfred von Richthofen. He was one of the most skilled fighter pilots of all time. He became known as "The Red Baron" because one of his favorite airplanes was painted bright red. He shot down 80 Allied aircraft during his career, which finally came to an end in 1918 when he died in the wreckage of his famous plane.

HANDLEY PAGE

ONLY EIGHT HANDLEY PAGE H.P. 42s were built between 1930 and 1931, but by the time they went out of service in 1940, they had flown great distances and had earned a place in the affection of crew and passengers alike. They were, in the words of their manufacturer, "the world's first airliners." Many of the passengers they carried said they were the most comfortable planes they ever flew in. Four H.P. 42s carried mail and passengers between Cairo, Egypt, and Karachi (then in India). The other four flew between London and Paris. All were given "H" names – Hannibal, Hadrian, Hanno, and Horsa were the eastern planes; Hercules, Horatius, Hengist, and Helena flew in Europe.

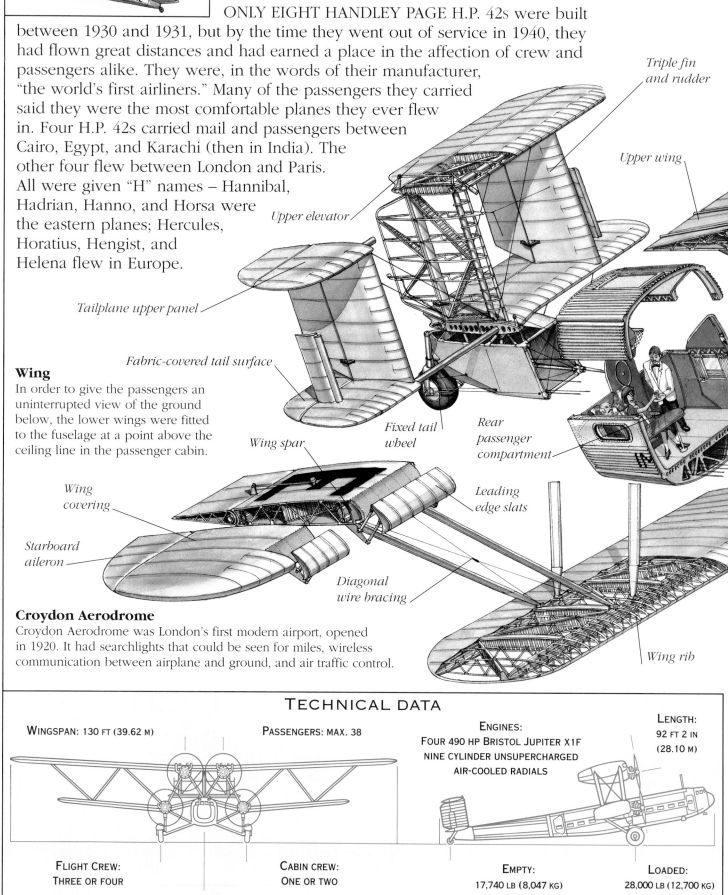

Triple fin and rudder

Upper wing

Upper elevator

Tailplane upper panel

Fabric-covered tail surface

Wing

In order to give the passengers an uninterrupted view of the ground below, the lower wings were fitted to the fuselage at a point above the ceiling line in the passenger cabin.

Wing spar

Fixed tail wheel

Rear passenger compartment

Wing covering

Starboard aileron

Leading edge slats

Diagonal wire bracing

Wing rib

Croydon Aerodrome

Croydon Aerodrome was London's first modern airport, opened in 1920. It had searchlights that could be seen for miles, wireless communication between airplane and ground, and air traffic control.

TECHNICAL DATA

WINGSPAN: 130 FT (39.62 M)

PASSENGERS: MAX. 38

ENGINES:
FOUR 490 HP BRISTOL JUPITER X1F
NINE CYLINDER UNSUPERCHARGED
AIR-COOLED RADIALS

LENGTH:
92 FT 2 IN
(28.10 M)

FLIGHT CREW:
THREE OR FOUR

CABIN CREW:
ONE OR TWO

EMPTY:
17,740 LB (8,047 KG)

LOADED:
28,000 LB (12,700 KG)

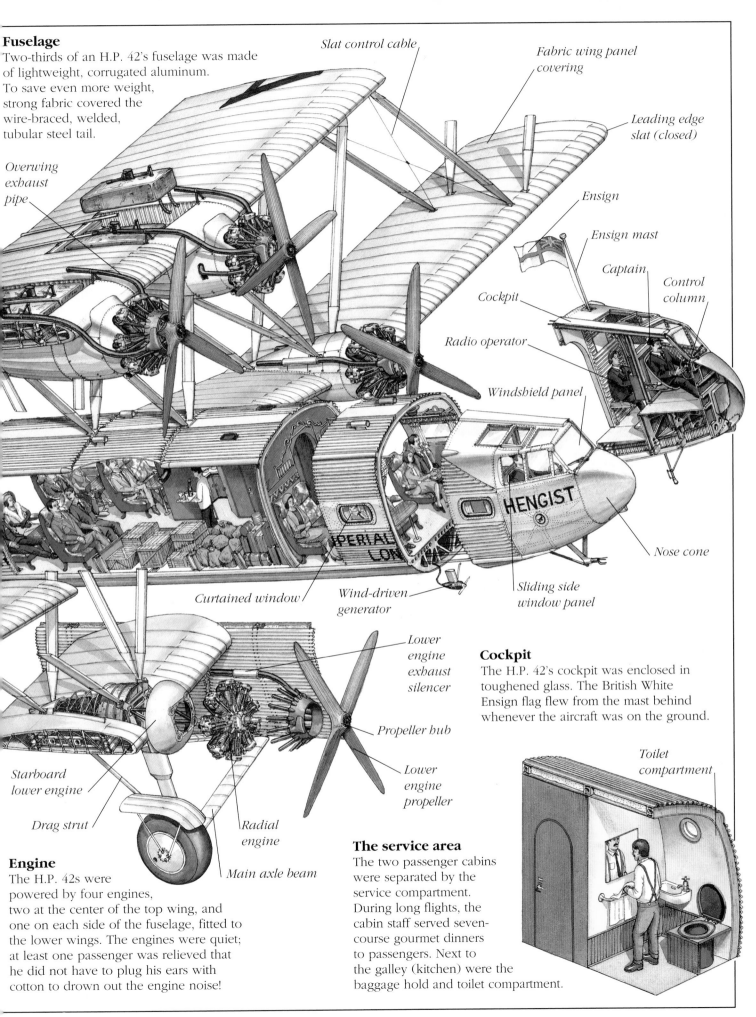

Fuselage
Two-thirds of an H.P. 42's fuselage was made of lightweight, corrugated aluminum. To save even more weight, strong fabric covered the wire-braced, welded, tubular steel tail.

Overwing exhaust pipe

Slat control cable

Fabric wing panel covering

Leading edge slat (closed)

Ensign

Ensign mast

Captain

Control column

Cockpit

Radio operator

Windshield panel

HENGIST

IPERIAL
LON

Curtained window

Wind-driven generator

Sliding side window panel

Nose cone

Lower engine exhaust silencer

Propeller hub

Lower engine propeller

Cockpit
The H.P. 42's cockpit was enclosed in toughened glass. The British White Ensign flag flew from the mast behind whenever the aircraft was on the ground.

Starboard lower engine

Drag strut

Radial engine

Main axle beam

Toilet compartment

Engine
The H.P. 42s were powered by four engines, two at the center of the top wing, and one on each side of the fuselage, fitted to the lower wings. The engines were quiet; at least one passenger was relieved that he did not have to plug his ears with cotton to drown out the engine noise!

The service area
The two passenger cabins were separated by the service compartment. During long flights, the cabin staff served seven-course gourmet dinners to passengers. Next to the galley (kitchen) were the baggage hold and toilet compartment.

BOEING 314

ONLY EIGHT YEARS after the Wright Brothers flew into aviation's history books, another American, Glenn Curtiss, skimmed in by making the first takeoff from water, in January 1911. The seaplane had been created. Perhaps the most famous seaplanes were the Boeing 314s, which first flew in 1938. In March 1939, California Clipper carried passengers from San Francisco to Singapore. In June of the same year, Atlantic Clipper made the first official transatlantic passenger flight. During World War II, the Clippers were used to ferry men and materials all over the world. By the time the war came to an end, the 314s had made over 4,100 transoceanic flights. After the war however, flying boats could not compete with the new planes being built. The Clippers were sold off and later scrapped.

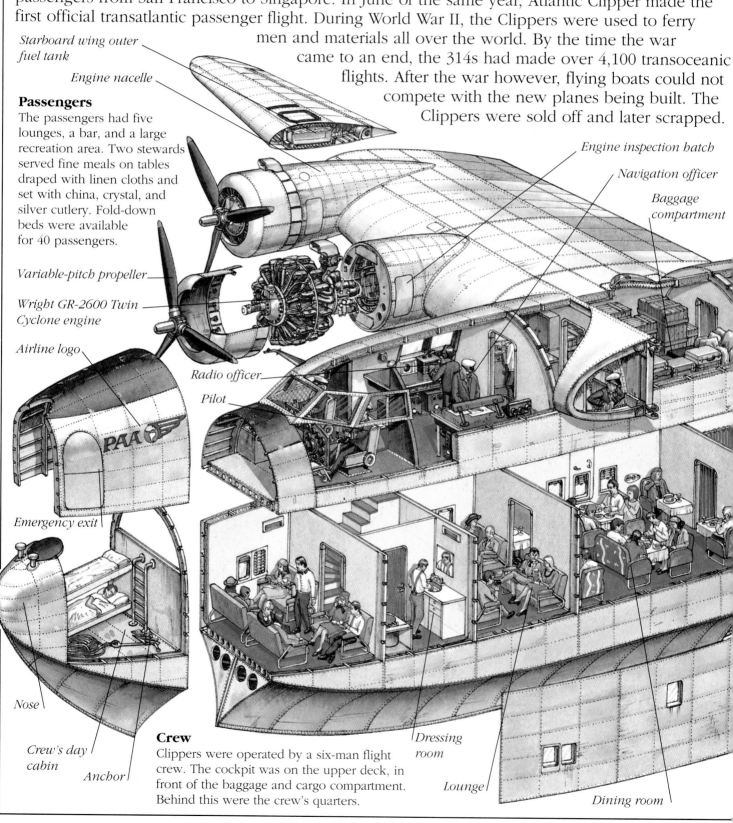

Starboard wing outer fuel tank

Engine nacelle

Passengers
The passengers had five lounges, a bar, and a large recreation area. Two stewards served fine meals on tables draped with linen cloths and set with china, crystal, and silver cutlery. Fold-down beds were available for 40 passengers.

Variable-pitch propeller

Wright GR-2600 Twin Cyclone engine

Airline logo

Radio officer

Pilot

Emergency exit

Nose

Crew's day cabin

Anchor

Engine inspection hatch

Navigation officer

Baggage compartment

Crew
Clippers were operated by a six-man flight crew. The cockpit was on the upper deck, in front of the baggage and cargo compartment. Behind this were the crew's quarters.

Dressing room

Lounge

Dining room

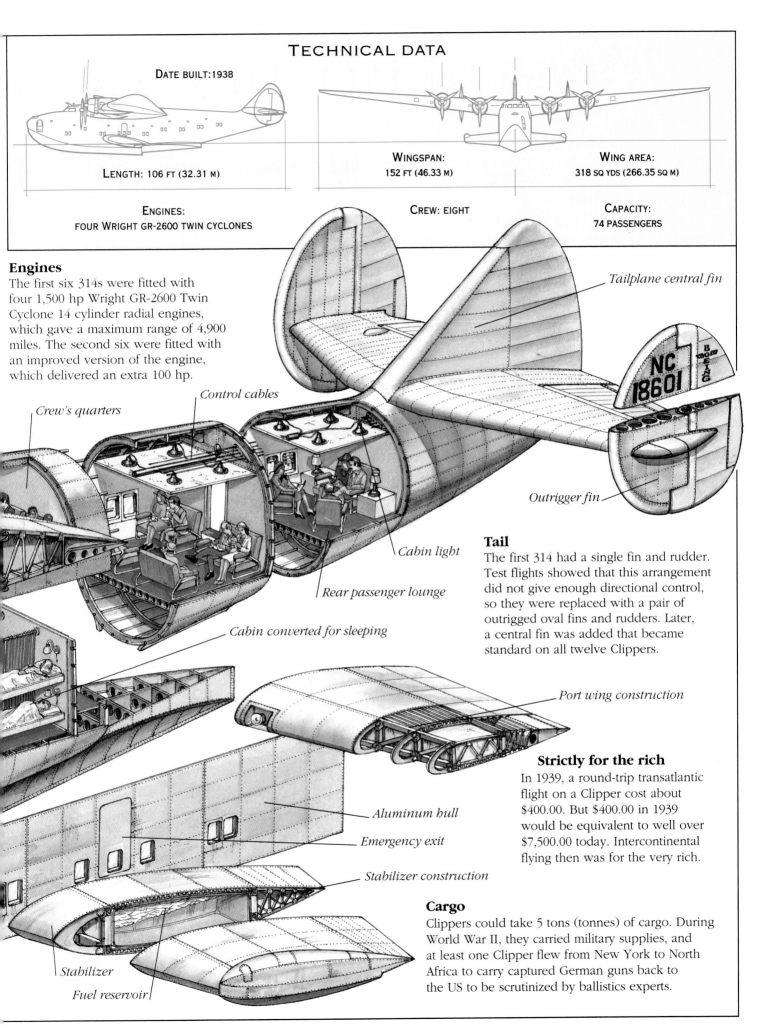

TECHNICAL DATA

DATE BUILT: 1938

LENGTH: 106 FT (32.31 M)

WINGSPAN:
152 FT (46.33 M)

WING AREA:
318 SQ YDS (266.35 SQ M)

ENGINES:
FOUR WRIGHT GR-2600 TWIN CYCLONES

CREW: EIGHT

CAPACITY:
74 PASSENGERS

Engines
The first six 314s were fitted with four 1,500 hp Wright GR-2600 Twin Cyclone 14 cylinder radial engines, which gave a maximum range of 4,900 miles. The second six were fitted with an improved version of the engine, which delivered an extra 100 hp.

Crew's quarters

Control cables

Tailplane central fin

Outrigger fin

Cabin light

Rear passenger lounge

Tail
The first 314 had a single fin and rudder. Test flights showed that this arrangement did not give enough directional control, so they were replaced with a pair of outrigged oval fins and rudders. Later, a central fin was added that became standard on all twelve Clippers.

Cabin converted for sleeping

Port wing construction

Aluminum hull

Emergency exit

Stabilizer construction

Stabilizer

Fuel reservoir

Strictly for the rich
In 1939, a round-trip transatlantic flight on a Clipper cost about $400.00. But $400.00 in 1939 would be equivalent to well over $7,500.00 today. Intercontinental flying then was for the very rich.

Cargo
Clippers could take 5 tons (tonnes) of cargo. During World War II, they carried military supplies, and at least one Clipper flew from New York to North Africa to carry captured German guns back to the US to be scrutinized by ballistics experts.

SPITFIRE

THE SPITFIRE CAME INTO BEING because the chief designer of the Supermarine Aviation Works was determined to build an aircraft that would win the famous Schneider Trophy Race, an international flying event held in the 1920s and 30s. His designs for a racing airplane gradually evolved into a fighter, and the prototype (first one) flew in March 1936. The plane was light and easy to fly. It performed so well in trials, exceeding all British requirements for fighter aircraft, that in June of the same year the first production models were ordered.

Perfect props
The first Spitfires had large, three-blade propellers. Later models had four- or even five-blade propellers.

Engine
Early Spitfires had Rolls-Royce Merlin I piston engines. The 1942 Mark IX, powered by a Merlin 60, could fly at 404 mph (650 km/h). Later models were fitted with the larger Griffin engine. One of the last Spitfires of all, the Mark XXI, was twice as powerful as the original Spitfire Mark I.

Big shots
The Spitfire Mark I was armed with eight machine guns. Later Spitfires usually had two 20-mm cannon and four machine guns.

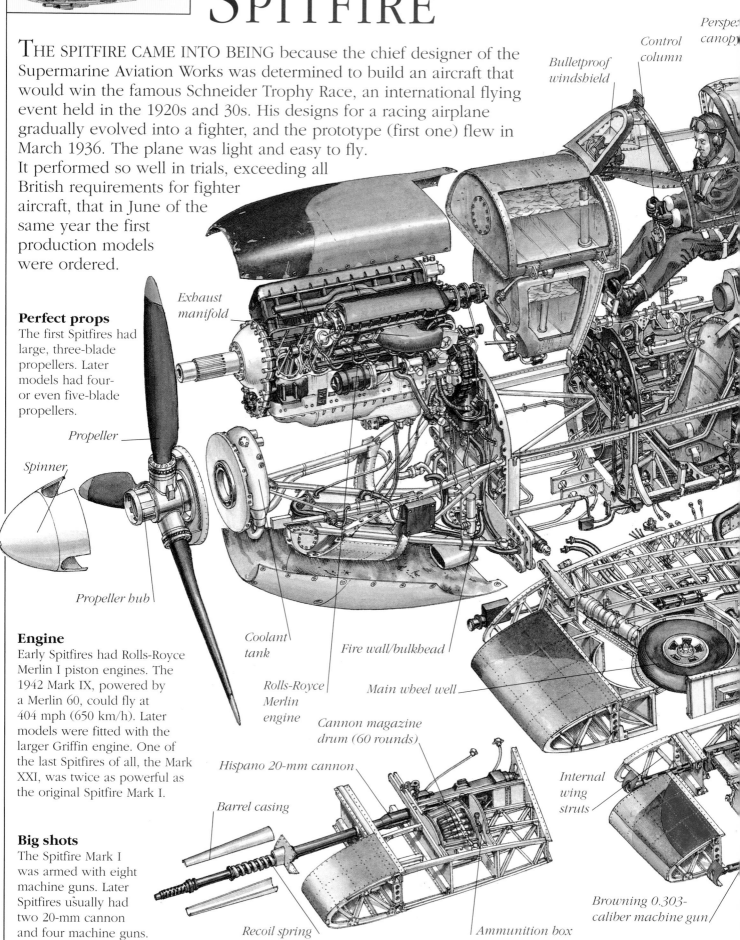

Perspex canopy

Control column

Bulletproof windshield

Exhaust manifold

Propeller

Spinner

Propeller hub

Coolant tank

Rolls-Royce Merlin engine

Fire wall/bulkhead

Main wheel well

Cannon magazine drum (60 rounds)

Hispano 20-mm cannon

Barrel casing

Internal wing struts

Recoil spring

Ammunition box

Browning 0.303-caliber machine gun

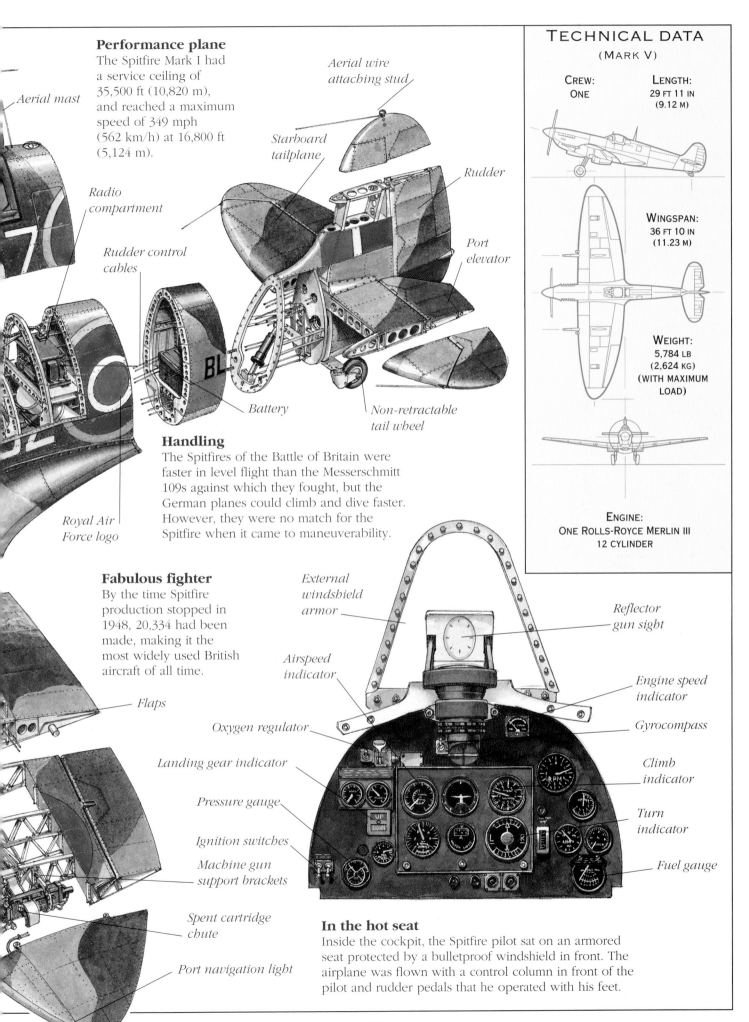

Performance plane
The Spitfire Mark I had a service ceiling of 35,500 ft (10,820 m), and reached a maximum speed of 349 mph (562 km/h) at 16,800 ft (5,124 m).

Aerial mast

Aerial wire attaching stud

Starboard tailplane

Rudder

Radio compartment

Rudder control cables

Port elevator

Battery

Non-retractable tail wheel

Royal Air Force logo

Handling
The Spitfires of the Battle of Britain were faster in level flight than the Messerschmitt 109s against which they fought, but the German planes could climb and dive faster. However, they were no match for the Spitfire when it came to maneuverability.

Fabulous fighter
By the time Spitfire production stopped in 1948, 20,334 had been made, making it the most widely used British aircraft of all time.

Flaps

External windshield armor

Reflector gun sight

Airspeed indicator

Engine speed indicator

Oxygen regulator

Gyrocompass

Landing gear indicator

Climb indicator

Pressure gauge

Turn indicator

Ignition switches

Machine gun support brackets

Fuel gauge

Spent cartridge chute

In the hot seat
Inside the cockpit, the Spitfire pilot sat on an armored seat protected by a bulletproof windshield in front. The airplane was flown with a control column in front of the pilot and rudder pedals that he operated with his feet.

Port navigation light

FLYING FORTRESS

IMAGINE A HUGE FORTRESS lifted off the ground and flying through the air. Bristling with guns and packed with bombs, it would be a sight to strike fear into any enemy. The US B-17 bomber was just such a sight. The mainstay of bombing operations in Europe during World War II, it was also widely used in the Pacific, the Middle East, and the Far East. The B-17 made its first appearance in 1935 as Boeing's prototype Model 299. It was given its official designation, B-17, after its trials for the US Army. The B-17G, which was introduced in 1943, was armed with twin machine guns in the chin, dorsal, ventral, and tail gun turrets plus two in the nose, one in the radio compartment, and one in each waist position.

Bombs

The B-17s normally carried a payload of 6,000 lb (2,724 kg) of bombs, but they could carry more than double that. The bombs were controlled by the bombardier who sat at the lip of the plane's nose.

Radio operator's compartment

Windshield

Good-luck mascot painting

Up front

The pilot and copilot sat alongside each other in the cramped cockpit. The glass surrounding it was tough, but not bulletproof.

Navigator's compartment

Bombardier

Copilot

Bomb-bay bulkhead

Dorsal gun turret

Bomb bay

Pilot

Navigator

Norden bombsight

Nose machine guns

Port main wheel

Bomb

Engines

The B-17G was powered by four Wright Cyclone engines. These gave it a maximum speed of 287 mph (462 km/h). Even early in its career, the B-17 made long-distance flights, including one from Miami to Buenos Aires – a distance of 5,260 miles (8,465 km).

Plexiglass frameless nose cone

Optically flat bomb-aiming panel

Detonator

High explosive

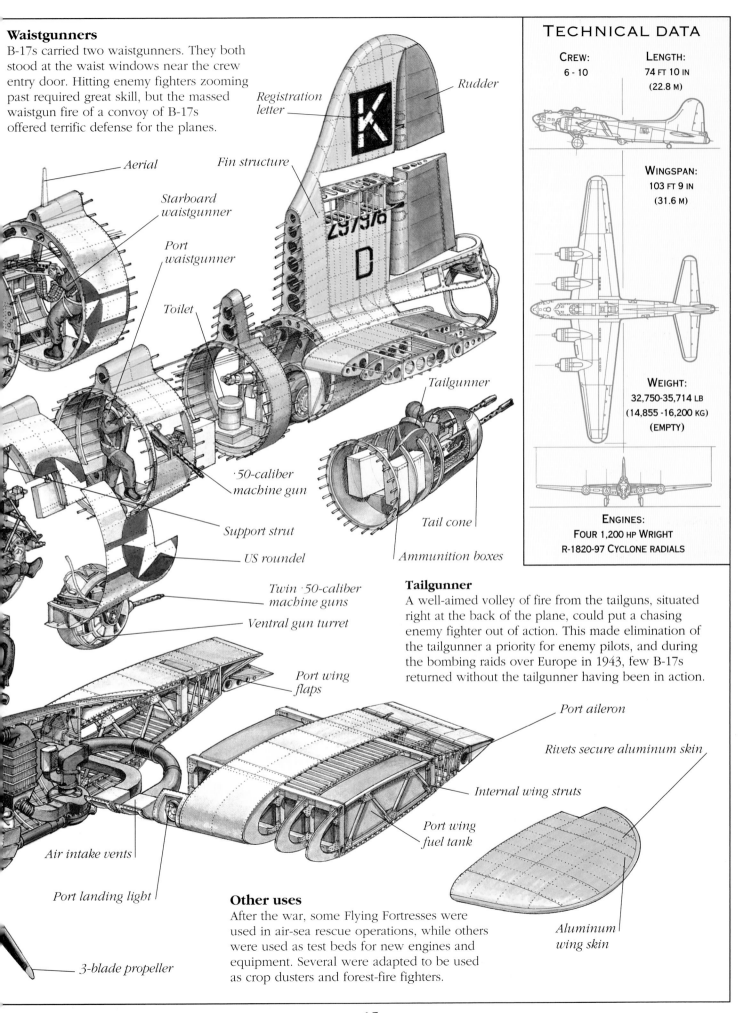

Waistgunners

B-17s carried two waistgunners. They both stood at the waist windows near the crew entry door. Hitting enemy fighters zooming past required great skill, but the massed waistgun fire of a convoy of B-17s offered terrific defense for the planes.

Rudder

Registration letter

Aerial

Fin structure

Starboard waistgunner

Port waistgunner

Toilet

Tailgunner

·50-caliber machine gun

Support strut

Tail cone

US roundel

Ammunition boxes

Twin ·50-caliber machine guns

Ventral gun turret

Port wing flaps

Tailgunner

A well-aimed volley of fire from the tailguns, situated right at the back of the plane, could put a chasing enemy fighter out of action. This made elimination of the tailgunner a priority for enemy pilots, and during the bombing raids over Europe in 1943, few B-17s returned without the tailgunner having been in action.

Port aileron

Rivets secure aluminum skin

Internal wing struts

Port wing fuel tank

Air intake vents

Port landing light

Other uses

After the war, some Flying Fortresses were used in air-sea rescue operations, while others were used as test beds for new engines and equipment. Several were adapted to be used as crop dusters and forest-fire fighters.

Aluminum wing skin

3-blade propeller

TECHNICAL DATA

CREW:
6 - 10

LENGTH:
74 FT 10 IN
(22.8 M)

WINGSPAN:
103 FT 9 IN
(31.6 M)

WEIGHT:
32,750-35,714 LB
(14,855 -16,200 KG)
(EMPTY)

ENGINES:
FOUR 1,200 HP WRIGHT
R-1820-97 CYCLONE RADIALS

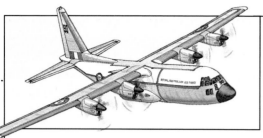

HERCULES

"YOU BUILD TOUGH AIRPLANES!" That's what the governor of Georgia said in 1954 after he had "launched" the first production C-130 Hercules by breaking a bottle of water over its nose. It had taken four tries to shatter the glass, and the Hercules wasn't even scratched. The Hercules is indeed tough. More than 1,700 have been produced in about 40 versions. They still roll off the production lines at the rate of about three a month. They are flown by more than 50 of the world's air forces and have proven their ruggedness over and over again, in war and at peace. The C-130 can land on sand, snow, rough terrain, and even aircraft carriers. There has even been a Hercules aerobatic team!

The cockpit
The pilot and copilot sit alongside each other at the front of the cockpit, which is extremely spacious. Behind them is the navigation station and the systems engineer's seat. The cockpit is equipped with rest bunks where the crew take turns sleeping during long flights.

Radar
The C-130, like all modern aircraft, is equipped with radar. When the radio waves sent out by the transmitter hit an object, they are reflected back to the radar station. The signal passes through a cathode-ray tube on which an image of what the radio beam has hit appears. Aircraft use radar to detect other aircraft, targets, and approaching bad weather.

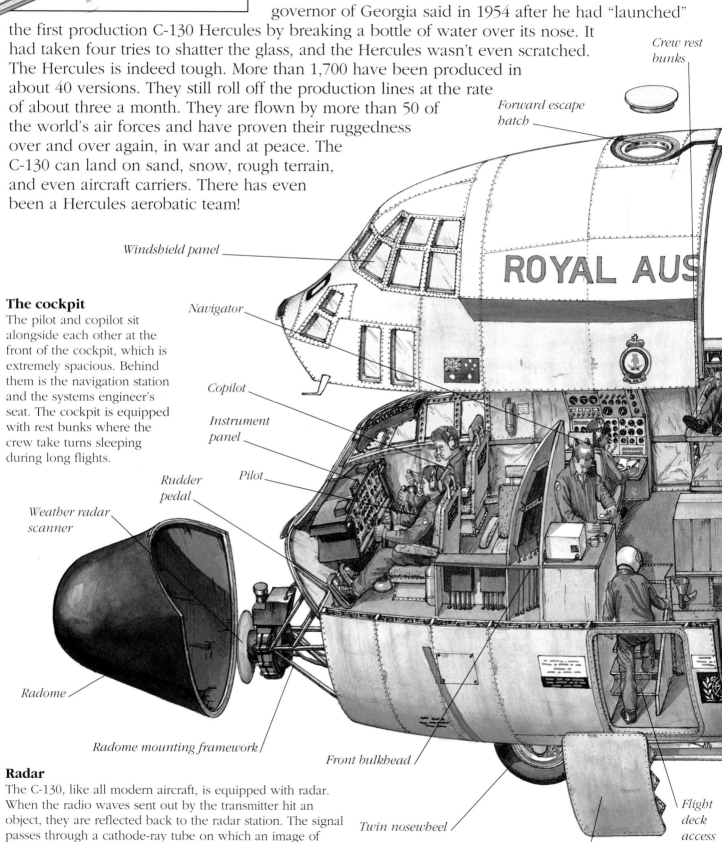

Crew rest bunks

Forward escape hatch

Windshield panel

Navigator

Copilot

Instrument panel

Pilot

Rudder pedal

Weather radar scanner

Radome

Radome mounting framework

Front bulkhead

Twin nosewheel

Crew entry door

Flight deck access ladder

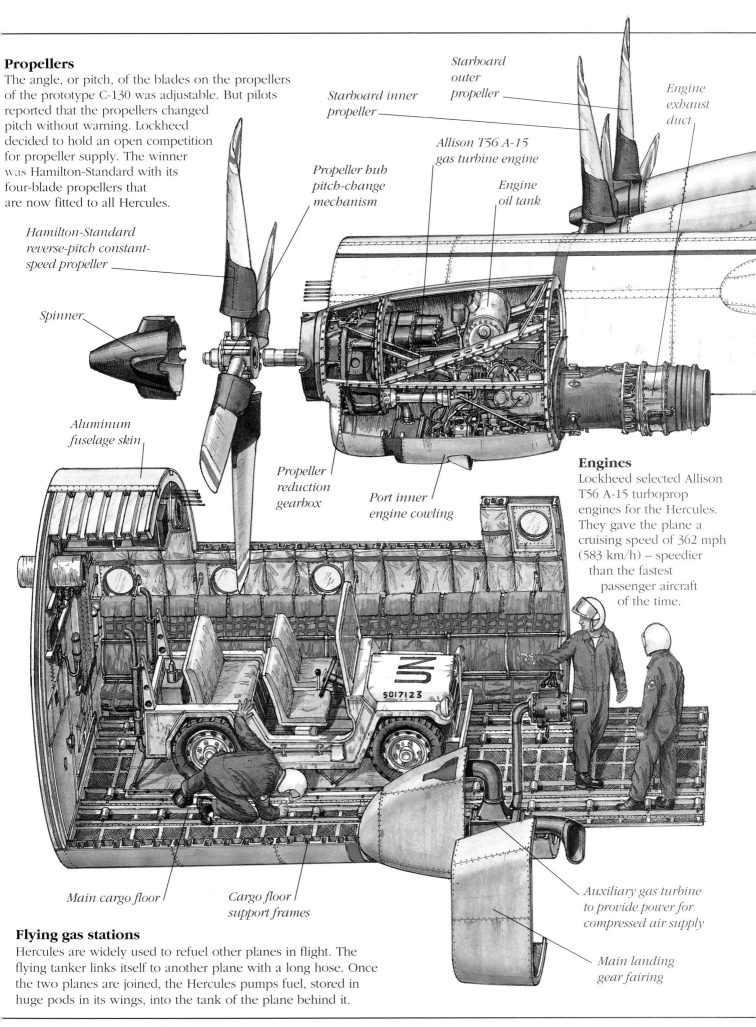

Propellers

The angle, or pitch, of the blades on the propellers of the prototype C-130 was adjustable. But pilots reported that the propellers changed pitch without warning. Lockheed decided to hold an open competition for propeller supply. The winner was Hamilton-Standard with its four-blade propellers that are now fitted to all Hercules.

Hamilton-Standard reverse-pitch constant-speed propeller

Spinner

Aluminum fuselage skin

Starboard inner propeller

Starboard outer propeller

Engine exhaust duct

Propeller hub pitch-change mechanism

Allison T56 A-15 gas turbine engine

Engine oil tank

Propeller reduction gearbox

Port inner engine cowling

Engines

Lockheed selected Allison T56 A-15 turboprop engines for the Hercules. They gave the plane a cruising speed of 362 mph (583 km/h) – speedier than the fastest passenger aircraft of the time.

Main cargo floor

Cargo floor support frames

Auxiliary gas turbine to provide power for compressed air supply

Main landing gear fairing

Flying gas stations

Hercules are widely used to refuel other planes in flight. The flying tanker links itself to another plane with a long hose. Once the two planes are joined, the Hercules pumps fuel, stored in huge pods in its wings, into the tank of the plane behind it.

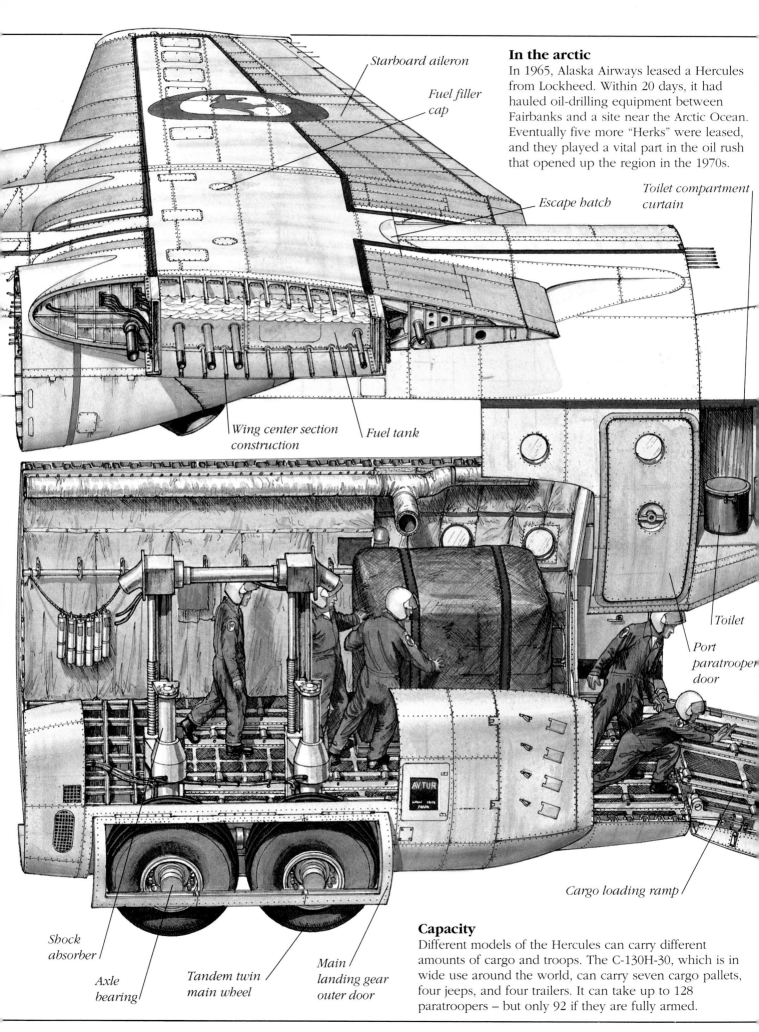

Starboard aileron

Fuel filler cap

In the arctic
In 1965, Alaska Airways leased a Hercules from Lockheed. Within 20 days, it had hauled oil-drilling equipment between Fairbanks and a site near the Arctic Ocean. Eventually five more "Herks" were leased, and they played a vital part in the oil rush that opened up the region in the 1970s.

Escape hatch

Toilet compartment curtain

Wing center section construction

Fuel tank

Toilet

Port paratrooper door

Cargo loading ramp

Shock absorber

Axle bearing

Tandem twin main wheel

Main landing gear outer door

Capacity
Different models of the Hercules can carry different amounts of cargo and troops. The C-130H-30, which is in wide use around the world, can carry seven cargo pallets, four jeeps, and four trailers. It can take up to 128 paratroopers – but only 92 if they are fully armed.

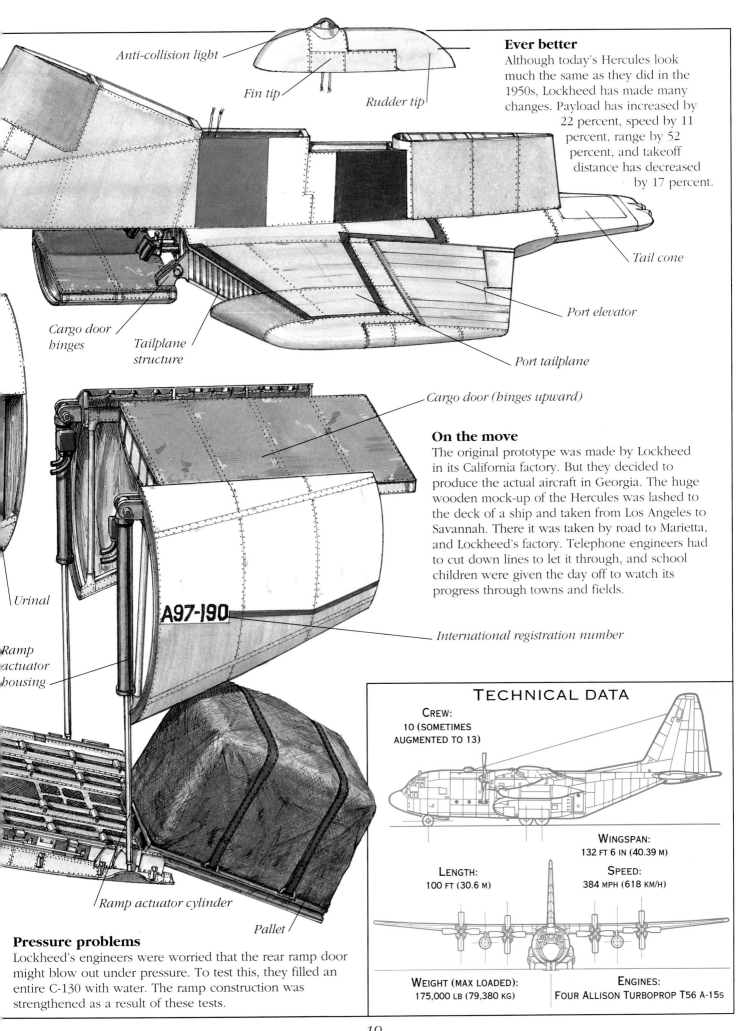

Anti-collision light

Fin tip

Rudder tip

Ever better

Although today's Hercules look much the same as they did in the 1950s, Lockheed has made many changes. Payload has increased by 22 percent, speed by 11 percent, range by 52 percent, and takeoff distance has decreased by 17 percent.

Tail cone

Cargo door hinges

Tailplane structure

Port elevator

Port tailplane

Cargo door (hinges upward)

On the move

The original prototype was made by Lockheed in its California factory. But they decided to produce the actual aircraft in Georgia. The huge wooden mock-up of the Hercules was lashed to the deck of a ship and taken from Los Angeles to Savannah. There it was taken by road to Marietta, and Lockheed's factory. Telephone engineers had to cut down lines to let it through, and school children were given the day off to watch its progress through towns and fields.

Urinal

A97-190

International registration number

Ramp actuator housing

TECHNICAL DATA

CREW:
10 (SOMETIMES AUGMENTED TO 13)

WINGSPAN:
132 FT 6 IN (40.39 M)

LENGTH:
100 FT (30.6 M)

SPEED:
384 MPH (618 KM/H)

Ramp actuator cylinder

Pallet

Pressure problems

Lockheed's engineers were worried that the rear ramp door might blow out under pressure. To test this, they filled an entire C-130 with water. The ramp construction was strengthened as a result of these tests.

WEIGHT (MAX LOADED):
175,000 LB (79,380 KG)

ENGINES:
FOUR ALLISON TURBOPROP T56 A-15S

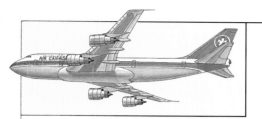

BOEING 747

IN 1960, THE WORLD'S
airlines carried more than 106 million passengers. By 1966,
this had mushroomed to 200 million. The volume of cargo
being carried by air also soared. As more and more airplanes
took to the skies, airports became more and more crowded,
and so, to absorb this dramatic increase, manufacturers
decided to try to make larger aircraft. The first of the wide-
bodied airplanes was Boeing's 747. It first flew on February
9, 1969. Less than a year later, it entered service on the
transatlantic route with Pan American airlines, carrying more
than 350 passengers from New York to London. With one
bold step, Boeing had doubled the capacity, power, and
weight of transportation aircraft. No wonder this mammoth
machine was called "Jumbo." The name stuck, and the 747
and its successors have all been
called jumbo jets.

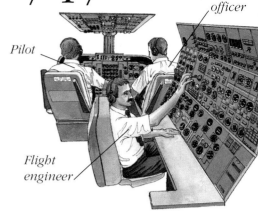

The flight deck
Most 747s are flown by a three-person crew
– pilot, first officer, and flight engineer. The
pilot and first officer sit next to each other,
with the flight engineer behind. The 747-400,
introduced in 1988, has a two-crew flight deck

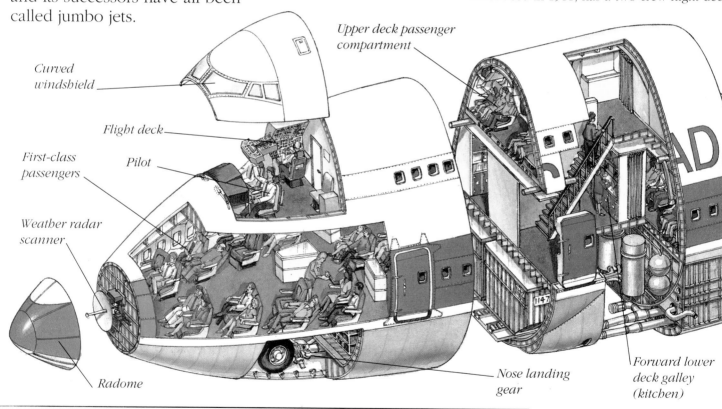

Curved
windshield

Upper deck passenger
compartment

Flight deck

First-class
passengers

Pilot

Weather radar
scanner

Nose landing
gear

Forward lower
deck galley
(kitchen)

Radome

TECHNICAL DATA

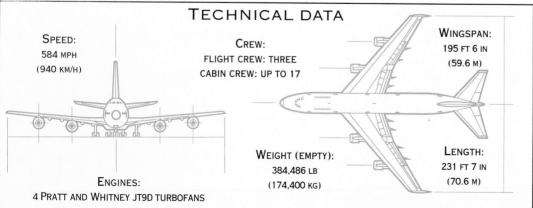

SPEED:
584 MPH
(940 KM/H)

CREW:
FLIGHT CREW: THREE
CABIN CREW: UP TO 17

WINGSPAN:
195 FT 6 IN
(59.6 M)

WEIGHT (EMPTY):
384,486 LB
(174,400 KG)

LENGTH:
231 FT 7 IN
(70.6 M)

ENGINES:
4 PRATT AND WHITNEY JT9D TURBOFANS

747 variations
747 variations include the 747S
(Special Purpose), which is 49
(15 m) shorter than the standar
747, but has a higher tail fin. It
carries more fuel and flies farth
than any other subsonic aircraf
One, on a delivery flight in
March 1976, was flown nonstop
from Seattle, Washington to
Cape Town, South Africa.

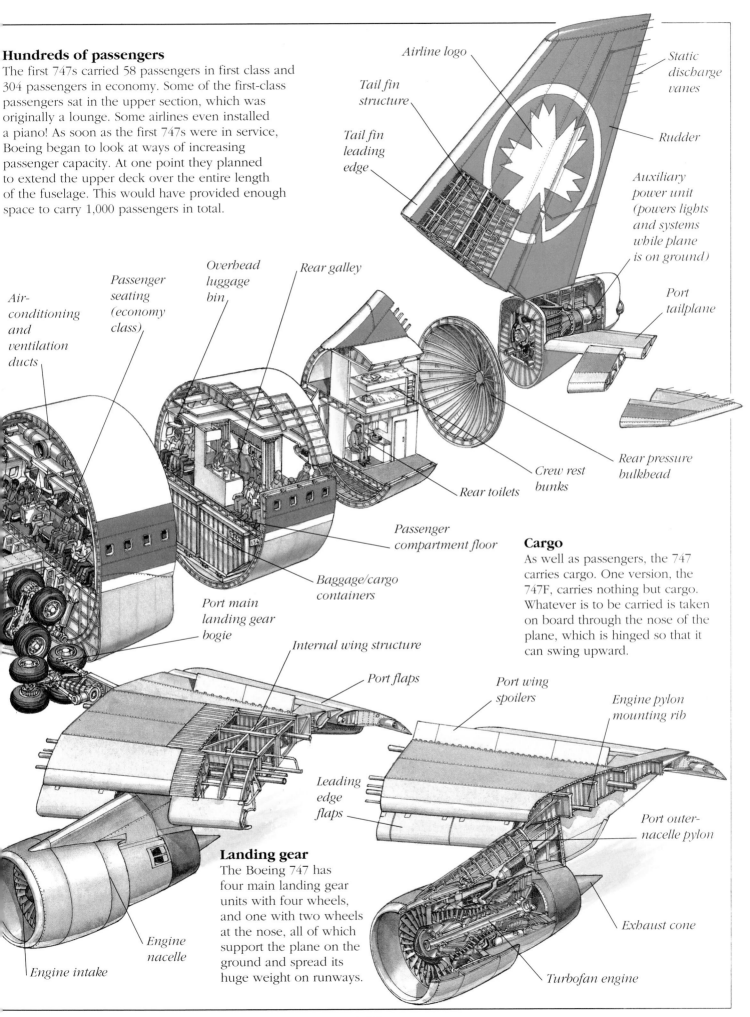

Hundreds of passengers

The first 747s carried 58 passengers in first class and 304 passengers in economy. Some of the first-class passengers sat in the upper section, which was originally a lounge. Some airlines even installed a piano! As soon as the first 747s were in service, Boeing began to look at ways of increasing passenger capacity. At one point they planned to extend the upper deck over the entire length of the fuselage. This would have provided enough space to carry 1,000 passengers in total.

Airline logo

Tail fin structure

Tail fin leading edge

Static discharge vanes

Rudder

Auxiliary power unit (powers lights and systems while plane is on ground)

Port tailplane

Overhead luggage bin

Rear galley

Passenger seating (economy class)

Air-conditioning and ventilation ducts

Rear pressure bulkhead

Crew rest bunks

Rear toilets

Passenger compartment floor

Cargo

As well as passengers, the 747 carries cargo. One version, the 747F, carries nothing but cargo. Whatever is to be carried is taken on board through the nose of the plane, which is hinged so that it can swing upward.

Baggage/cargo containers

Port main landing gear bogie

Internal wing structure

Port flaps

Port wing spoilers

Engine pylon mounting rib

Leading edge flaps

Port outer-nacelle pylon

Landing gear

The Boeing 747 has four main landing gear units with four wheels, and one with two wheels at the nose, all of which support the plane on the ground and spread its huge weight on runways.

Exhaust cone

Engine nacelle

Turbofan engine

Engine intake

PIPER CHIEFTAIN

LIGHT AIRCRAFT ARE USED FOR CROP SPRAYING, air-sea rescue, and fire fighting. They also often carry small numbers of passengers to places unsuitable for large aircraft. For many years, one of the leading light aircraft manufacturers has been the Piper Corporation in the US. This company has produced an enormous variety of small airplanes, ranging from single-seaters that can fly so low the pilots can almost lean out of the cockpit and touch the treetops, to sophisticated luxury jets that can whisk up to ten people from place to place. Piper aircraft, including the Chieftain PA-31, are popular with airlines around the world. In fact, they are so successful that Piper set up its own airline division in 1981.

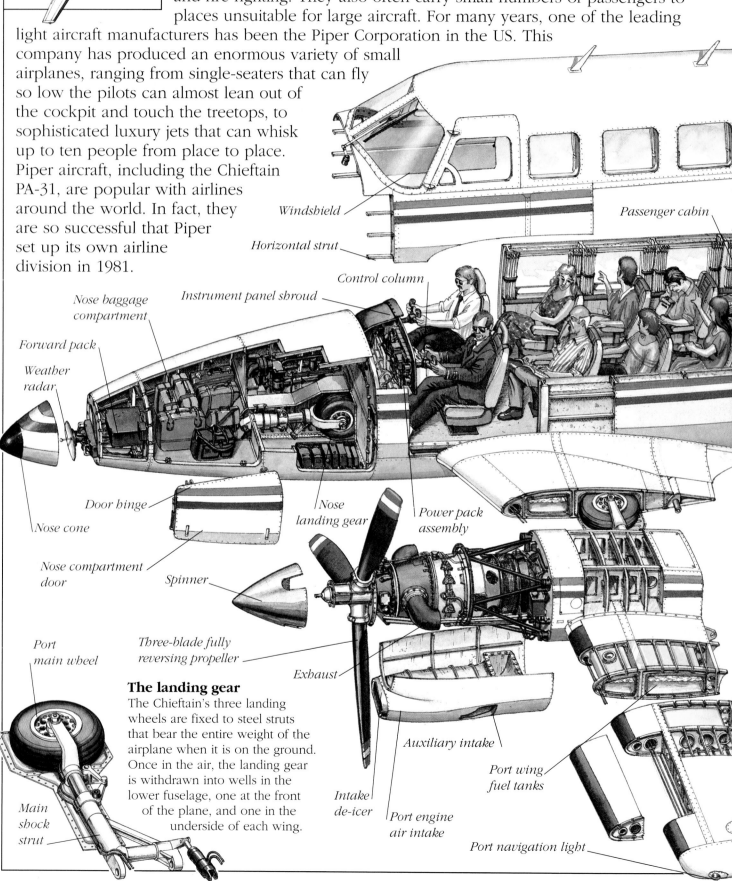

Windshield

Passenger cabin

Horizontal strut

Control column

Instrument panel shroud

Nose baggage compartment

Forward pack

Weather radar

Door hinge

Nose cone

Nose compartment door

Spinner

Nose landing gear

Power pack assembly

Port main wheel

Three-blade fully reversing propeller

Exhaust

The landing gear
The Chieftain's three landing wheels are fixed to steel struts that bear the entire weight of the airplane when it is on the ground. Once in the air, the landing gear is withdrawn into wells in the lower fuselage, one at the front of the plane, and one in the underside of each wing.

Auxiliary intake

Port wing fuel tanks

Main shock strut

Intake de-icer

Port engine air intake

Port navigation light

22

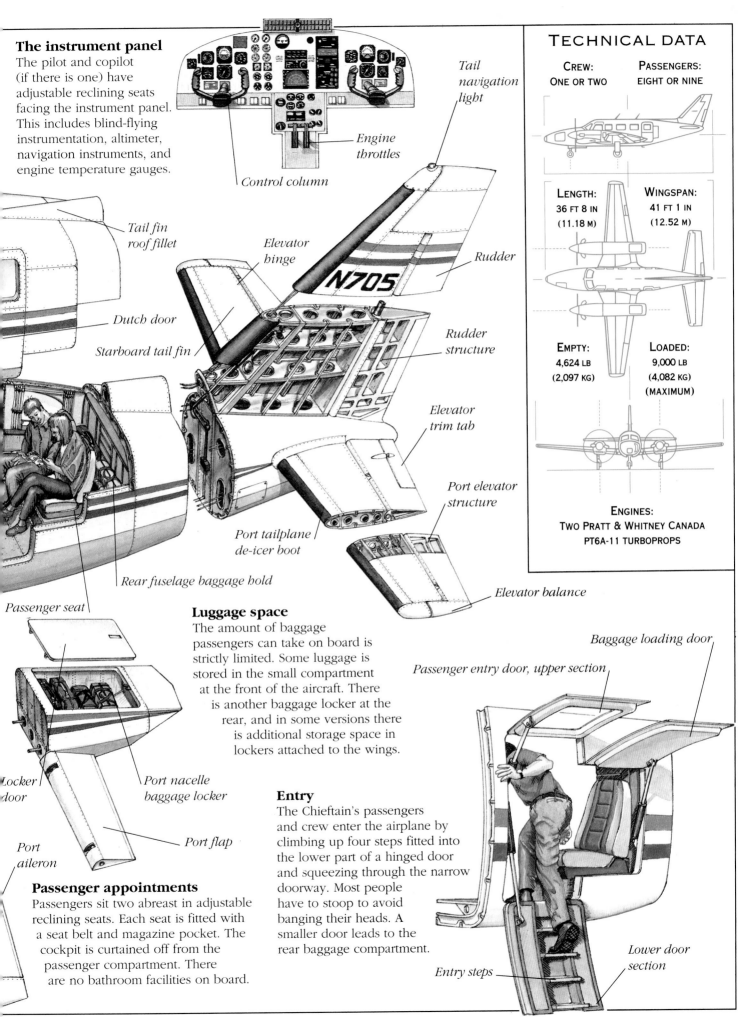

The instrument panel
The pilot and copilot (if there is one) have adjustable reclining seats facing the instrument panel. This includes blind-flying instrumentation, altimeter, navigation instruments, and engine temperature gauges.

Engine throttles

Control column

Tail fin roof fillet

Elevator hinge

Dutch door

Starboard tail fin

Tail navigation light

Rudder

Rudder structure

N705

Elevator trim tab

Port elevator structure

Port tailplane de-icer boot

Rear fuselage baggage hold

Elevator balance

Passenger seat

Luggage space
The amount of baggage passengers can take on board is strictly limited. Some luggage is stored in the small compartment at the front of the aircraft. There is another baggage locker at the rear, and in some versions there is additional storage space in lockers attached to the wings.

Baggage loading door

Passenger entry door, upper section

Locker door

Port nacelle baggage locker

Port flap

Port aileron

Entry
The Chieftain's passengers and crew enter the airplane by climbing up four steps fitted into the lower part of a hinged door and squeezing through the narrow doorway. Most people have to stoop to avoid banging their heads. A smaller door leads to the rear baggage compartment.

Passenger appointments
Passengers sit two abreast in adjustable reclining seats. Each seat is fitted with a seat belt and magazine pocket. The cockpit is curtained off from the passenger compartment. There are no bathroom facilities on board.

Entry steps

Lower door section

TECHNICAL DATA

CREW: ONE OR TWO

PASSENGERS: EIGHT OR NINE

LENGTH: 36 FT 8 IN (11.18 M)

WINGSPAN: 41 FT 1 IN (12.52 M)

EMPTY: 4,624 LB (2,097 KG)

LOADED: 9,000 LB (4,082 KG) (MAXIMUM)

ENGINES:
TWO PRATT & WHITNEY CANADA PT6A-11 TURBOPROPS

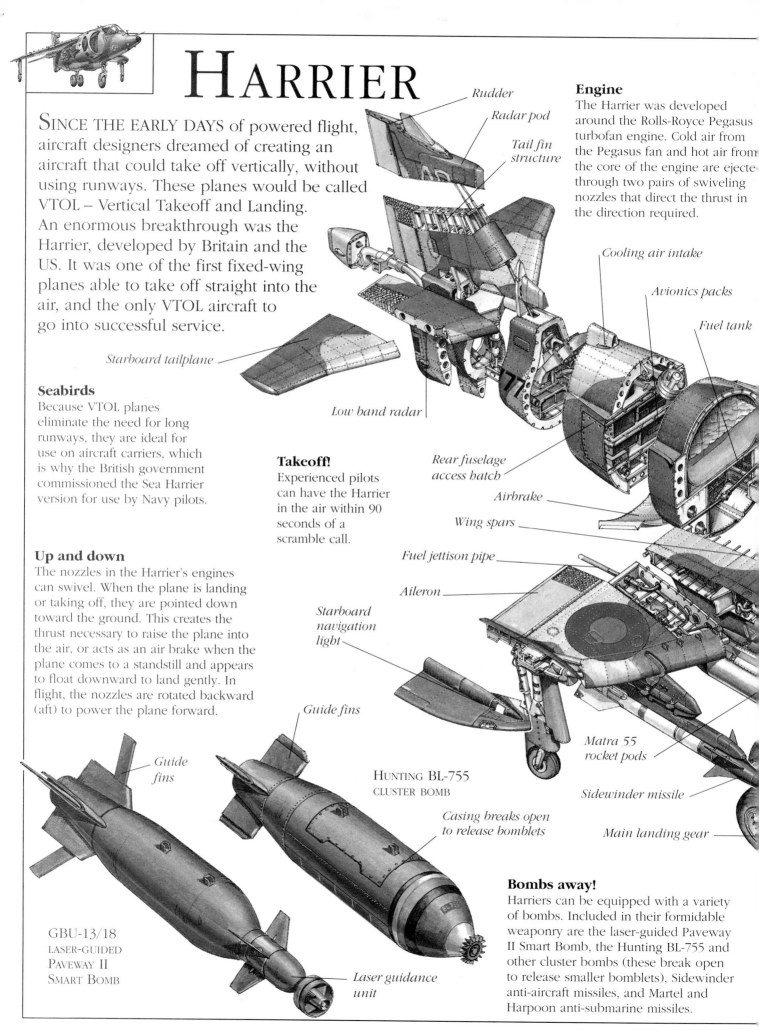

HARRIER

SINCE THE EARLY DAYS of powered flight, aircraft designers dreamed of creating an aircraft that could take off vertically, without using runways. These planes would be called VTOL – Vertical Takeoff and Landing. An enormous breakthrough was the Harrier, developed by Britain and the US. It was one of the first fixed-wing planes able to take off straight into the air, and the only VTOL aircraft to go into successful service.

Starboard tailplane

Seabirds

Because VTOL planes eliminate the need for long runways, they are ideal for use on aircraft carriers, which is why the British government commissioned the Sea Harrier version for use by Navy pilots.

Up and down

The nozzles in the Harrier's engines can swivel. When the plane is landing or taking off, they are pointed down toward the ground. This creates the thrust necessary to raise the plane into the air, or acts as an air brake when the plane comes to a standstill and appears to float downward to land gently. In flight, the nozzles are rotated backward (aft) to power the plane forward.

Rudder

Radar pod

Tail fin structure

Engine

The Harrier was developed around the Rolls-Royce Pegasus turbofan engine. Cold air from the Pegasus fan and hot air from the core of the engine are ejected through two pairs of swiveling nozzles that direct the thrust in the direction required.

Cooling air intake

Avionics packs

Fuel tank

Low band radar

Takeoff!

Experienced pilots can have the Harrier in the air within 90 seconds of a scramble call.

Rear fuselage access hatch

Airbrake

Wing spars

Fuel jettison pipe

Aileron

Starboard navigation light

Guide fins

Guide fins

HUNTING BL-755
CLUSTER BOMB

Casing breaks open to release bomblets

Matra 55 rocket pods

Sidewinder missile

Main landing gear

GBU-13/18
LASER-GUIDED
PAVEWAY II
SMART BOMB

Laser guidance unit

Bombs away!

Harriers can be equipped with a variety of bombs. Included in their formidable weaponry are the laser-guided Paveway II Smart Bomb, the Hunting BL-755 and other cluster bombs (these break open to release smaller bomblets), Sidewinder anti-aircraft missiles, and Martel and Harpoon anti-submarine missiles.

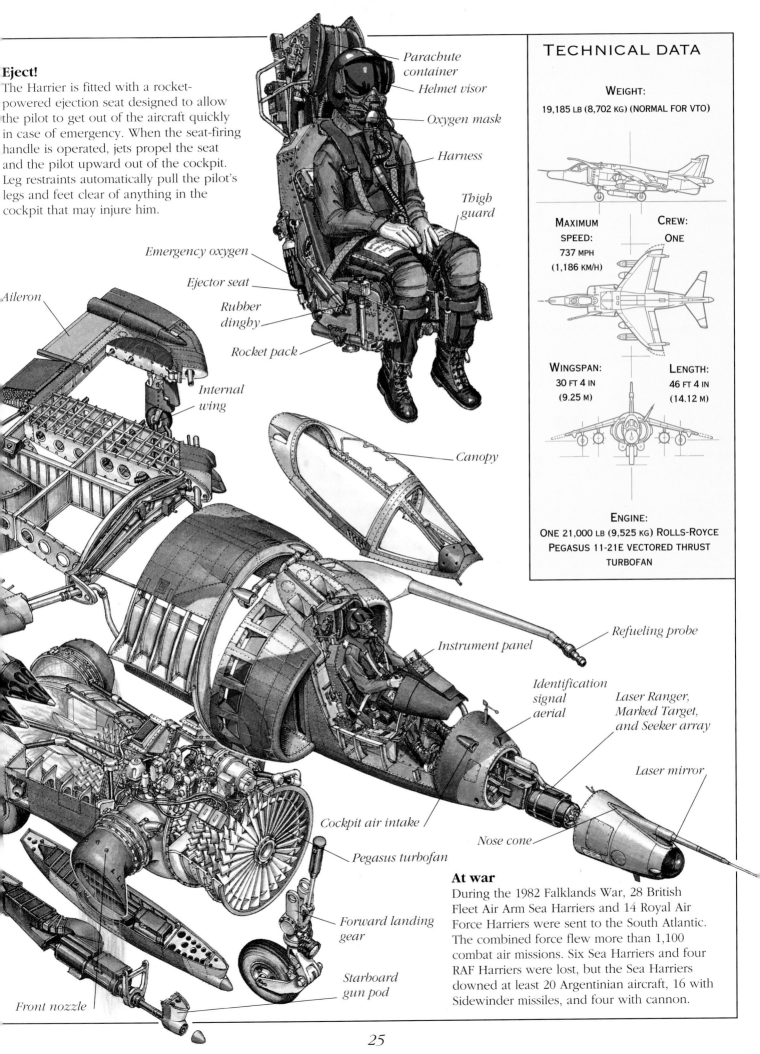

Eject!

The Harrier is fitted with a rocket-powered ejection seat designed to allow the pilot to get out of the aircraft quickly in case of emergency. When the seat-firing handle is operated, jets propel the seat and the pilot upward out of the cockpit. Leg restraints automatically pull the pilot's legs and feet clear of anything in the cockpit that may injure him.

Parachute container

Helmet visor

Oxygen mask

Harness

Thigh guard

Emergency oxygen

Ejector seat

Rubber dinghy

Rocket pack

Aileron

Internal wing

Canopy

TECHNICAL DATA

WEIGHT:
19,185 LB (8,702 KG) (NORMAL FOR VTO)

MAXIMUM SPEED:
737 MPH
(1,186 KM/H)

CREW:
ONE

WINGSPAN:
30 FT 4 IN
(9.25 M)

LENGTH:
46 FT 4 IN
(14.12 M)

ENGINE:
ONE 21,000 LB (9,525 KG) ROLLS-ROYCE PEGASUS 11-21E VECTORED THRUST TURBOFAN

Refueling probe

Instrument panel

Identification signal aerial

Laser Ranger, Marked Target, and Seeker array

Laser mirror

Cockpit air intake

Nose cone

Pegasus turbofan

Forward landing gear

Starboard gun pod

Front nozzle

At war

During the 1982 Falklands War, 28 British Fleet Air Arm Sea Harriers and 14 Royal Air Force Harriers were sent to the South Atlantic. The combined force flew more than 1,100 combat air missions. Six Sea Harriers and four RAF Harriers were lost, but the Sea Harriers downed at least 20 Argentinian aircraft, 16 with Sidewinder missiles, and four with cannon.

CONCORDE

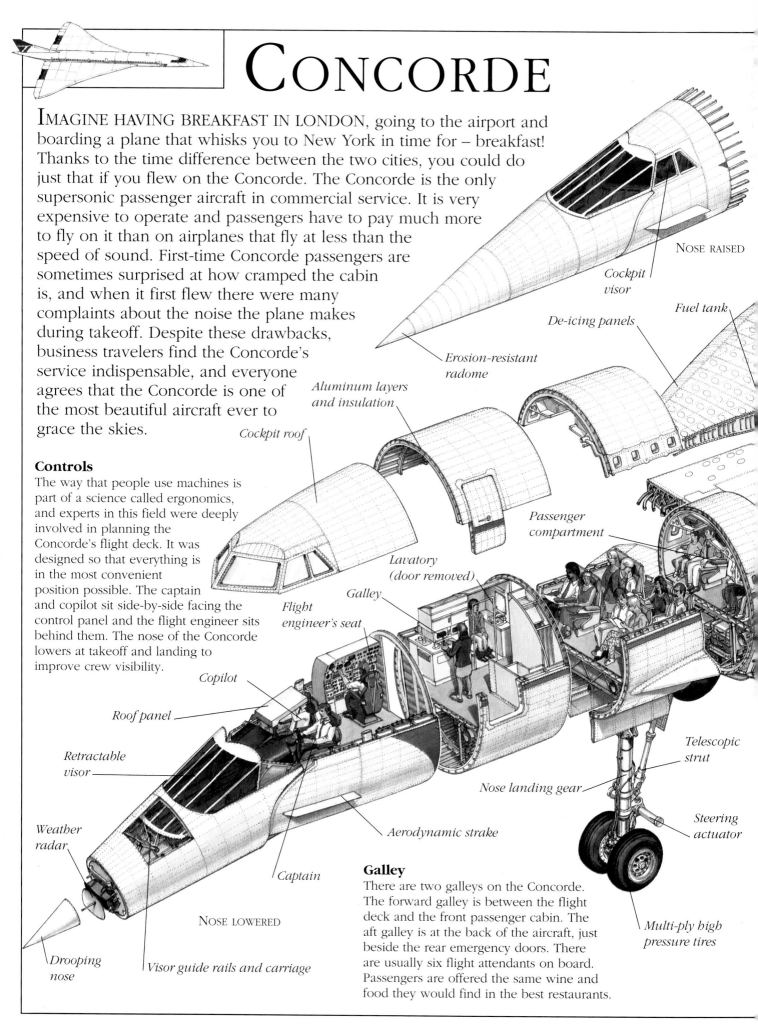

IMAGINE HAVING BREAKFAST IN LONDON, going to the airport and boarding a plane that whisks you to New York in time for – breakfast! Thanks to the time difference between the two cities, you could do just that if you flew on the Concorde. The Concorde is the only supersonic passenger aircraft in commercial service. It is very expensive to operate and passengers have to pay much more to fly on it than on airplanes that fly at less than the speed of sound. First-time Concorde passengers are sometimes surprised at how cramped the cabin is, and when it first flew there were many complaints about the noise the plane makes during takeoff. Despite these drawbacks, business travelers find the Concorde's service indispensable, and everyone agrees that the Concorde is one of the most beautiful aircraft ever to grace the skies.

Controls

The way that people use machines is part of a science called ergonomics, and experts in this field were deeply involved in planning the Concorde's flight deck. It was designed so that everything is in the most convenient position possible. The captain and copilot sit side-by-side facing the control panel and the flight engineer sits behind them. The nose of the Concorde lowers at takeoff and landing to improve crew visibility.

Galley

There are two galleys on the Concorde. The forward galley is between the flight deck and the front passenger cabin. The aft galley is at the back of the aircraft, just beside the rear emergency doors. There are usually six flight attendants on board. Passengers are offered the same wine and food they would find in the best restaurants.

Nose raised

Cockpit visor

De-icing panels

Fuel tank

Erosion-resistant radome

Aluminum layers and insulation

Cockpit roof

Passenger compartment

Lavatory (door removed)

Galley

Flight engineer's seat

Copilot

Roof panel

Retractable visor

Weather radar

Captain

Aerodynamic strake

Nose landing gear

Telescopic strut

Steering actuator

Multi-ply high pressure tires

NOSE LOWERED

Drooping nose

Visor guide rails and carriage

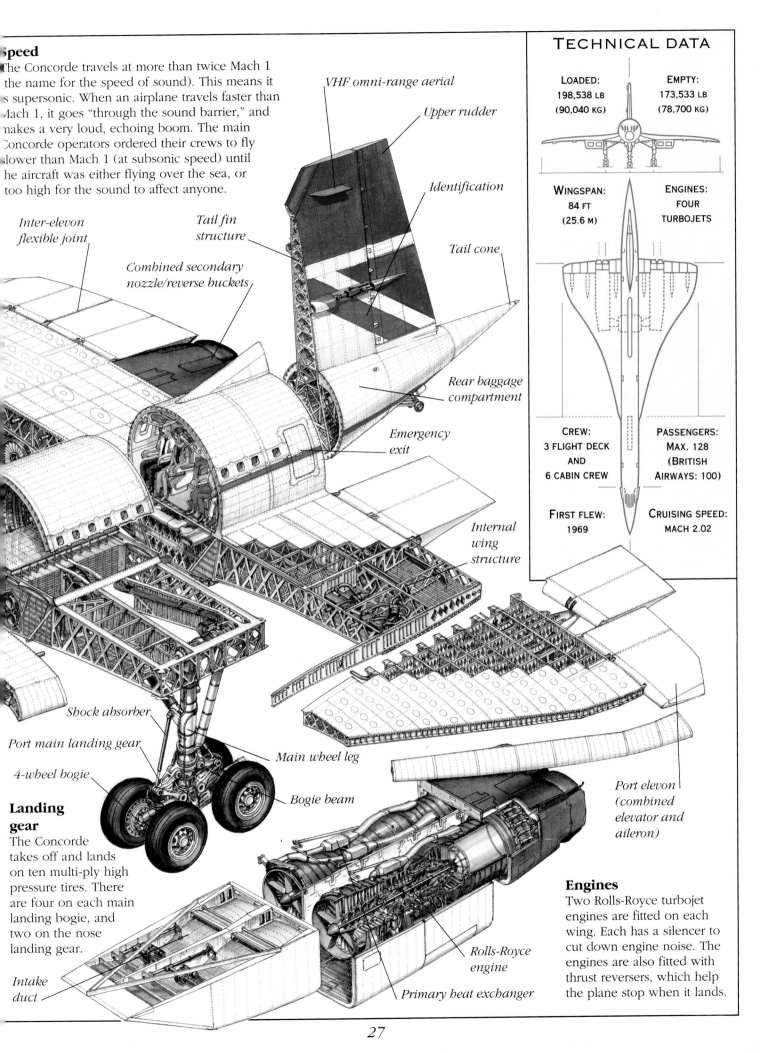

Speed

The Concorde travels at more than twice Mach 1 (the name for the speed of sound). This means it is supersonic. When an airplane travels faster than Mach 1, it goes "through the sound barrier," and makes a very loud, echoing boom. The main Concorde operators ordered their crews to fly slower than Mach 1 (at subsonic speed) until the aircraft was either flying over the sea, or too high for the sound to affect anyone.

Inter-elevon flexible joint

Tail fin structure

Combined secondary nozzle/reverse buckets

VHF omni-range aerial

Upper rudder

Identification

Tail cone

Rear baggage compartment

Emergency exit

Internal wing structure

Shock absorber

Port main landing gear

4-wheel bogie

Main wheel leg

Bogie beam

Landing gear

The Concorde takes off and lands on ten multi-ply high pressure tires. There are four on each main landing bogie, and two on the nose landing gear.

Intake duct

Port elevon (combined elevator and aileron)

Rolls-Royce engine

Primary heat exchanger

Engines

Two Rolls-Royce turbojet engines are fitted on each wing. Each has a silencer to cut down engine noise. The engines are also fitted with thrust reversers, which help the plane stop when it lands.

27

AIRCRAFT TIMELINE

In 1900, POWERED FLIGHT was only a fantasy. But in 1903, Orville Wright made the first flight in a heavier-than-air, powered machine. Today his plane would fit in a small corner of a C-130 Hercules, but flight has become a reality to virtually everyone. Here are some more milestones in the story of flight.

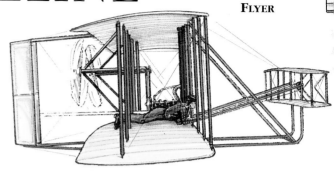

1903 WRIGHT FLYER

1918 FOKKER D.VII

1917 FOKKER DR.1

1930 HANDLEY-PAGE HP.42

1927 RYAN SPIRIT OF ST. LOUIS

1930 JUNKERS JU.52

Aluminum skin

1933 LOCKHEED VEGA

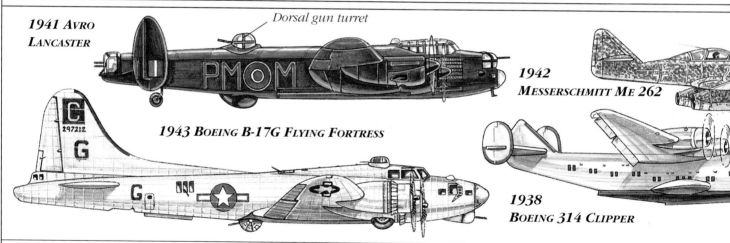

1941 AVRO LANCASTER

Dorsal gun turret

1943 BOEING B-17G FLYING FORTRESS

1942 MESSERSCHMITT ME 262

1938 BOEING 314 CLIPPER

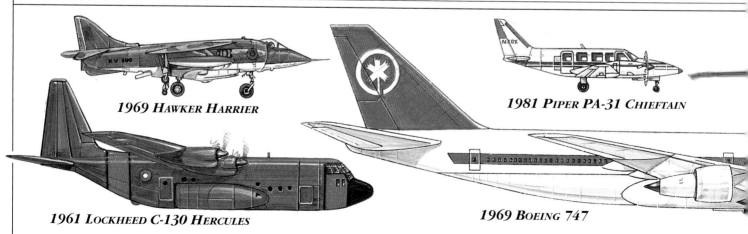

1969 HAWKER HARRIER

1981 PIPER PA-31 CHIEFTAIN

1961 LOCKHEED C-130 HERCULES

1969 BOEING 747

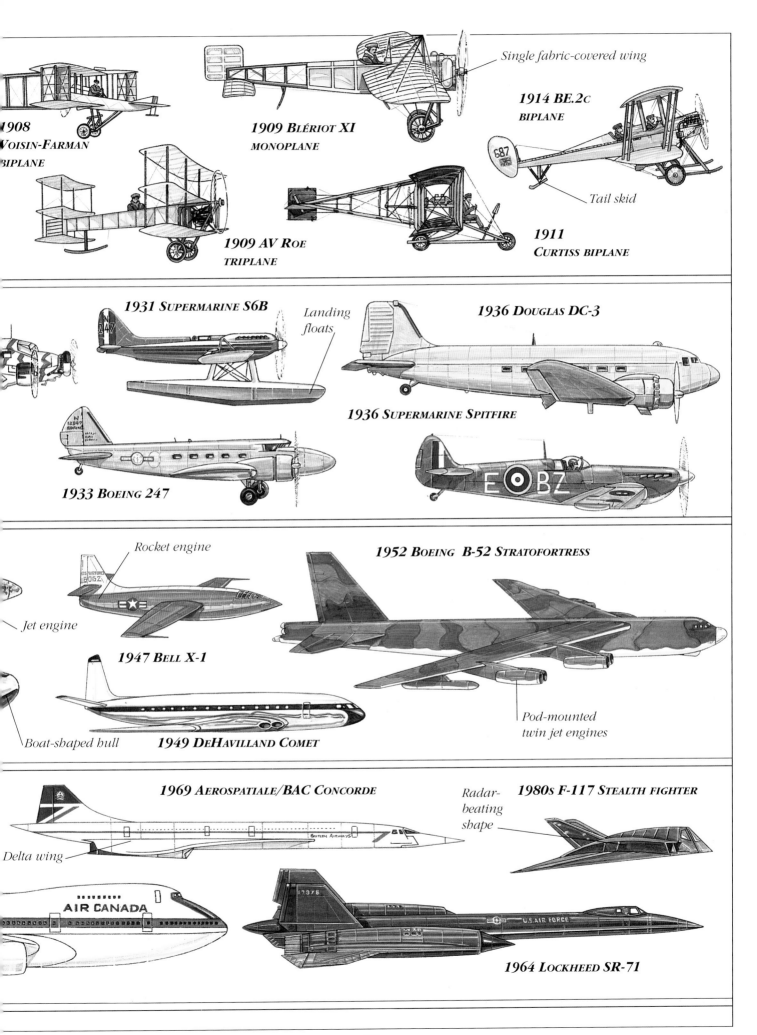

1908 VOISIN-FARMAN BIPLANE

1909 BLÉRIOT XI MONOPLANE

Single fabric-covered wing

1914 BE.2C BIPLANE

Tail skid

1909 AV ROE TRIPLANE

1911 CURTISS BIPLANE

1931 SUPERMARINE S6B

Landing floats

1936 DOUGLAS DC-3

1936 SUPERMARINE SPITFIRE

1933 BOEING 247

Rocket engine

1952 BOEING B-52 STRATOFORTRESS

Jet engine

1947 BELL X-1

1949 DEHAVILLAND COMET

Boat-shaped hull

Pod-mounted twin jet engines

1969 AEROSPATIALE/BAC CONCORDE

Radar-beating shape

1980S F-117 STEALTH FIGHTER

Delta wing

AIR CANADA

U.S. AIR FORCE

1964 LOCKHEED SR-71

GLOSSARY

Aileron
A movable surface hinged to the trailing edge of a plane's wing, to control roll.

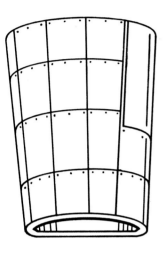

Airfoil

Airfoil
A shaped structure that causes lift when propelled through the air. A wing, propeller, rotor blade, and tailplane are all airfoils.

Airspeed indicator
An instrument that measures the speed of an aircraft in flight.

Air traffic control
The ground-based system that directs the movement of aircraft.

Altimeter
The instrument that records the height at which an aircraft is flying.

Autopilot
An electronic device that automatically maintains an aircraft in steady flight.

Biplane
An airplane with two sets of wings, one fixed above the other.

Bogie
The wheel assembly on the main landing leg.

Bulkhead
A solid partition that separates one part of an airplane from another.

Cantilever
A beam or other structure that is supported at one end only.

Cockpit
The compartment in an aircraft that houses the pilot and crew.

Control surface
A movable surface that, when moved, changes an aircraft's angle or direction of flight.

Copilot
The second pilot.

Delta wing
A triangular or near-triangular shaped wing, with the trailing edge forming the flat base of the triangle. The Concorde has delta wings.

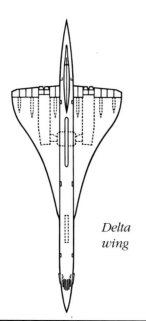

Delta wing

Drag
The resistance of air against moving objects.

Elevator
A control surface hinged to the back of the tailplane that controls climb and descent.

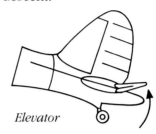

Elevator

Fin
The fixed vertical surface of a plane's tail unit that controls roll and yaw.

Flap
A surface hinged to the trailing edge of the wings that can be lowered partially, to increase lift, or fully, to increase drag.

Flight deck
The crew compartment in a cabin aircraft.

Flight recorder
A crash-proof device that continually notes the speed, height, control-surface position, and other important aspects of an airplane in flight.

Flying boat
An airplane that can land on and take off from water due to its boat-shaped hull.

Flying wires
The wires of a non-cantilever wing that bear the load of the wing in flight.

Fuselage
The body of an aircraft.

Galley
The compartment where all supplies necessary for food and drink to be served during a flight are stored.

Glide slope
The descent path along which an aircraft comes in to land.

Gyrocompass
A nonmagnetic compass that indicates true north.

Inertial navigation system
A system that continuously measures changes in an airplane's speed and direction and feeds the information into a computer that determines an aircraft's precise position.

Instrument landing system
The system that guides a pilot when landing a plane in poor visibility with two sets of radio beams transmitted from the ground alongside a runway.

Jet engine
An engine that draws in air and burns fuel to emit a stream of hot gas that creates the thrust that propels an aircraft forward.

Jet engine

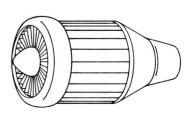

Leading edge
An airfoil's front edge.

Lift
The force generated by an airfoil at a 90-degree angle to the airstream flowing past it.

Mach 1
The speed of sound (741 mph [1,193 km/h]).

Magnetic compass
An instrument that contains a magnet that always settles pointing to magnetic north.

Pitch
The movement of an aircraft around an imaginary line extending from wingtip to wingtip, that results in the tail moving up and down. Pitch is controlled by elevators on the tailplane.

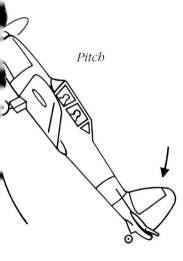

Pitch

Power plant
An aircraft's engine or engines.

Propeller
The engine-driven rotating blades that create the thrust that pushes an aircraft forward.

Propeller

Radar
Radio **D**etection **a**nd **R**anging: the navigation system that uses beams of directed radio waves to locate and detect objects.

Radome
The protective covering that houses radar antenna, made from a material through which radar waves can pass.

Reverse pitch
A set of an airplane's propeller blades that exerts a backward thrust to slow an aircraft after landing.

Reverse thrust
The effect caused by deflecting jet exhaust forward to produce a rearward thrust that slows an airplane after it lands.

Roll
The movement of an airplane around the imaginary line that runs down the center of the aircraft from nose to tail. The tilting, sideways motion is controlled by the ailerons.

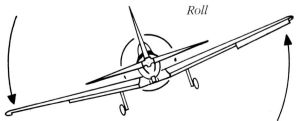

Roll

Rudder
The movable control surface hinged to the tail fin that controls yaw.

Slat
An extra, small aileron fitted to the leading edge of an airfoil to increase lift.

Slot
The gap between the slat and the main airfoil surface.

Span
The distance from wingtip to wingtip.

Spoiler
The control surface of an aircraft's wings that disturbs air flow over the wing and destroys lift. In use, a spoiler increases drag and slows an aircraft.

Supersonic aircraft
Planes that fly at speeds greater than Mach 1.

Tailplane
The horizontal airfoil surface of the tail unit that provides stability along the length of an aircraft. The tailplane may be fixed or adjustable.

Thrust
The force generated by propellers or jet engine flow that propels a plane through the air.

Thrust reversers
The parts of the engine that deflect exhaust gases forward to slow an aircraft when landing.

Trailing edge
An airfoil's rear edge.

Turbofan
A jet engine in which the bulk of the air intake by-passes the turbine and is discharged as a cold jet.

Turbojet
A jet engine in which the entire air intake passes through the combustion chamber and is discharged as a hot jet.

Turboprop
A gas-turbine engine that drives a propeller.

VTOL
Vertical **T**ake**o**ff and **L**anding.

VTOL

Wing
The principal supporting surface on both sides of an aircraft.

Yaw
The swiveling movement to right and left that can be controlled by the rudder on the tail fin.

Yaw

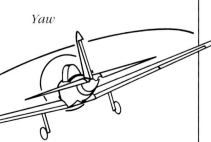

INDEX

A

airliner, first, 8
anti-aircraft/submarine
    missiles, 24, 25

B

Battle of Britain, 13
Boeing
    314, 10-11
    747, 20-21
    747-400, 20
    747F, 21
    747SP, 20
    B-17, 14-15
    B-17G, 14
bombardiers, 14
bomber airplanes
    Boeing B-17,
    14-15
    Hawker Harrier,
    24-25
bombs, 14, 24

C

C-130 Hercules, 16-19
C-130H Hercules, 18
cannons, 12
cargo
    Boeing 314, 11
    Boeing 747, 21
    C-130H-30
    Hercules, 18
Clippers, 10, 11
cluster bombs, 24
cockpit
    Boeing 314, 10
    Boeing B-17, 14
    C-130 Hercules,
    16
    Handley Page
    H.P. 42, 9
    Spitfire, 13
Concorde, 26-27
Crew
    Boeing 314, 10
    Boeing 747, 20
    C-130 Hercules,
    16
Croydon Aerodrome,
    8

E

ejection seat, 25
engines
    Allison, 17
    Griffin, 12
    on Handley Page
    H.P. 42, 9
    on Hawker
    Harrier, 24
    Rolls-Royce
    Merlin, 12
    Rolls-Royce
    Pegasus, 24
    Rolls-Royce
    turbojet, 26
    Wright Cyclone,
    14
    Wright GR-2600, 11

F

Falklands War, 25
fighter airplanes
    Fokker Dr. 1, 6-7
    Fokker *Eindecker*,
    6
    Spitfire, 12-13
flight deck
    Boeing 747, 20
    Concorde, 26
flying boats, 10
Flying Fortress, 14-15
flying tankers, 17
Fokker Dr. 1, 6-7
Fokker *Eindecker*, 6
fuselage
    Handley Page
    H.P. 42, 9

G

galleys
    Concorde, 26
    Handley Page
    H.P. 42, 9
guns, *see* machine guns

H

Handley Page H.P. 42, 8-9
Harrier, 24-25
Hawker Harrier, 24-25
Hercules, 16-19

I

Instrument panel
    Piper Chieftain
    PA-31, 23
    Spitfire, 13
interrupter gear, 7

J

Jumbo Jets, 20

L

landing gear/wheels
    Boeing 747, 21
    Concorde, 27
    Piper Chieftain
    PA-31, 22
light aircraft, 22
Lockheed C-130 Hercules,
    16-19
long-distance flights,
    14, 20

M

Mach 1, 27
machine guns
    Boeing B-17, 14
    Fokker Dr. 1, 6-7
    Spitfire, 12

P

passenger airplanes
    Boeing 747, 20-21
    Concorde, 26-27
    Handley Page
    H.P. 42, 8-9
passenger facilities on
    board
    Boeing 314, 10
    Boeing 747, 21
    Concorde, 26
    Handley Page
    H.P. 42, 9
    Piper Chieftain
    PA-31, 23
Piper Chieftain PA-31,
    22-23
propellers
    C-130 Hercules, 17
    Fokker Dr. 1, 6
    Spitfire, 12

R

radar, 16
Red Baron, 7
refueling in mid-air, 17
Richthofen, Baron
    Manfred von, 7

S

Schneider Trophy race, 12
Sea Harrier, 24, 25
seaplanes, 10
service area
    Handley Page
    H.P. 42, 9
speed
    Boeing 314, 11
    Boeing 747, 20
    Boeing B-17, 14
    Concorde, 27
    C-130 Hercules, 17
    Spitfire, 13
speed of sound, 27
Spitfire, 12-13
supersonic aircraft, 26

T

tailgunners, 15
triplanes, 6-7

V

VTOL (Vertical Takeoff
    and Landing), 24

W

waistgunners, 15
wide-bodied airplanes, 20
wings
    Fokker Dr. 1, 6
    Handley Page
    H.P. 42, 8

Acknowledgments

Dorling Kindersley would like
to thank the following people
who helped in the preparation
of this book:

Constance Novis for editorial
support
Lynn Bresler for the index
Boeing International Corporation
Additional artwork by Brihton
Illustration (pages 28-29)
Line artworks by John See